Smiling Stan, the Pedicab Man

Once there was a man named Stan.
He had a pedicab
and a big, big smile.
Stan took people across town.

"Thank you, Stan,"
the people said.
"Thank you for the ride
in your pedicab.
Thank you for your smile.
You make us very happy."

But one day, Stan and his pedicab were gone.

"Where is Stan?" the people asked. "Where is our happy pedicab man?"

Days went by.
No Stan!
The people were very sad.

Then a new taxicab
came to town.
The driver had a big, big smile.
Yes! The driver was Stan!

"No more pedicab!"
said Stan.
"Now I have a new taxicab.
Come for a ride!"

"Thank you, Stan!"
said the people.
"You make us very happy!"